Theos Friends' Programme

Theos is a religion and society think tank wh[...]
opinion about the role of faith and belief in s[...]

We were launched in November 2006 with t[...]
Dr Rowan Williams and the Cardinal Archbish[...]
Cardinal Cormac Murphy-O'Connor.

We provide

- high-quality research, reports and publications;
- an events programme;
- news, information and analysis to media companies,
  parliamentarians and other opinion formers.

We can only do this with your help!

Theos Friends receive complimentary copies of all Theos publications, invitations
to selected events and monthly email bulletins.

Theos Associates receive all the benefits of Friends and in addition are invited
to attend an exclusive annual dinner with the Theos Director and team.

If you would like to become a Friend or an Associate, please visit
www.theosthinktank.co.uk or detach or photocopy the form below, and send
it with a cheque to Theos for the relevant amount. Thank you.

Yes, I would like to help change public opinion!
I enclose a cheque payable to Theos for: ☐ **£60** (Friend) ☐ **£300** (Associate)

☐ Please send me information on how to give by standing order/direct debit

Name _____

Address _____

_____ Postcode _____

Email _____

Tel _____

Data Protection Theos will use your personal data to inform you of its activities.
If you prefer not to receive this information please tick here. ☐

*By completing you are consenting to receiving communications by telephone and email.
Theos will not pass on your details to any third party.*

Please return this form to:
Theos | 77 Great Peter Street | London | SW1P 2EZ
S: 97711   D: 36701

Theos✦

Theos – clear thinking on religion and society

Theos is a think tank working in the area of religion, politics and society. We aim to inform debate around questions of faith and secularism and the related subjects of values and identity. We were launched in November 2006, and our first report 'Doing God'; a Future for Faith in the Public Square, written by Nick Spencer, examined the reasons why faith will play an increasingly significant role in public life.

what Theos stands for

In our post-secular age, interest in spirituality is increasing across Western culture. We believe that it is impossible to understand the modern world without an understanding of religion. We also believe that much of the debate about the role and place of religion has been unnecessarily emotive and ill-informed. We reject the notion of any possible 'neutral' perspective on these issues.

what Theos works on

Theos conducts research, publishes reports, and runs debates, seminars and lectures on the intersection of religion, politics and society in the contemporary world. We also provide regular comment for print and broadcast media. Recent areas of analysis include multiculturalism, Christian education, religious liberty and the future of religious representation in the House of Lords. Future areas of focus will include questions of values in economic policy and practice and the role of religion in international affairs.

what Theos provides

In addition to our independently driven work, Theos provides research, analysis and advice to individuals and organisations across the private, public and not-for-profit sectors. Our unique position within the think tank sector means that we have the capacity to develop proposals that carry values – with an eye to demonstrating what really works.

what Theos believes

Theos was launched with the support of the Archbishop of Canterbury and the Cardinal Archbishop of Westminster, but it is independent of any particular denomination. We are an ecumenical Christian organisation, committed to the belief that religion in general and Christianity in particular has much to offer for the common good of society as a whole. We are committed to the traditional creeds of the Christian faith and draw on social and political thought from a wide range of theological traditions. We also work with many non-Christian and non-religious individuals and organisations.

From Goodness to God

Why Religion Makes Sense of our Moral Commitments

Angus Ritchie

Published by Theos in 2012
© Theos

ISBN 978-0-9562182-9-2

Some rights reserved – see copyright licence for details
For further information and subscription details please contact:

Theos
Licence Department
77 Great Peter Street
London
SW1P 2EZ

T 020 7828 7777
E hello@theosthinktank.co.uk
www.theosthinktank.co.uk

contents

acknowledgements

This report is based on my D.Phil. thesis and, in consequence, a considerable debt of gratitude is owed to Ralph Walker and Sabina Lovibond for their time and wisdom as doctoral supervisors. I would also like to thank Mark Harris for suggesting that I base a report upon this body of work and Elizabeth Oldfield and Nick Spencer whose patient guidance has enabled this to happen.

The funding for the report has come from the *Contending Modernities* programme at the University of Notre Dame – a project that is (among other things) exploring how different religious and secular worldviews negotiate a common life. Thanks are due to R. Scott Appleby and Vincent Rougeau for making possible both this report, and the wider partnership between *Contending Modernities*, Theos and the Contextual Theology Centre. There is more information on the programme at http://blogs.nd.edu/contendingmodernities.

Angus Ritchie
November 2012

foreword

Offer the view, in public, that belief in God gives you a better foundation for understanding, explaining and justifying human moral convictions than atheism does, and you risk looks of doubt, derision and disgust. The reason for this lies, in part, in the potential for confusion in this matter, which is why Angus Ritchie takes time at the start of this essay to explain what he is *not* saying.

From Goodness to God does not argue that only theists are good, or have a reason to be good, or know what being good involves. Nor does it argue that religious believers have some special access to the true moral compass, say, through their scriptures or personal revelation, one which others are denied. Rather, its claim is that theistic belief is able to explain why human beings' moral awareness and convictions actually say something true about morality. Put another way, it contends that belief in God is the best foundation for moral reasoning and for moral realism.

Even assuming you agree with moral realism – the belief that when we talk about morality we are talking about an objective reality rather than just our personal and subjective opinions, a position that Ritchie defends in his first chapter – this claim is still liable to raise eyebrows. So widespread is the New Atheist rhetoric that 'religious morality' is somehow a contradiction in terms, that many people who have not taken time to think through the matter are in danger of actually believing it.

As Ritchie argues, although atheism – the understanding of a universe that is free of purpose and design, let alone divine love and justice, in which humans are an accident of evolution by natural selection – might be able to explain the emergence of a rudimentary group-based ethic, this bears little resemblance to widespread human intuitions of what is right and wrong, and cannot, in any case, claim to be anything more than a survival strategy, useful until it no longer is. Moral reasoning based on atheism doesn't look like the morality with which most of us, including atheists, are familiar, and it doesn't even have much claim to be objectively true.

Moral reasoning based on belief in God, by contrast, in particular the God of classical theism, has something surer to offer. More precisely, such a belief offers a good explanation for the evolution (the essay has no qualms over the truth of natural selection) of moral animals such as ourselves, with our intuition of moral truth, our capacity for moral reasoning, and our desire to construct moral societies.

This is a big claim and *From Goodness to God* is a short essay. It does, however, have a much more substantial piece of work standing behind it, namely the author's *From Morality to Metaphysics: The Theistic Implications of our Moral Commitments* which is published by Oxford University Press. Readers eager for more detail are advised to go there.

From Goodness to God is not a comprehensive argument for the truth of theism, let alone Christianity. It is, however, an attempt to answer some of the more egregious atheistic claims and to show how belief in God, rather than being irrational, is the most rational foundation we have for our moral commitments.

Nick Spencer
Director of Research, Theos

introduction

religious reasoning in the public square

> Anyone truly interested in morality – in the principles of behaviour that allow people to flourish – should be open to new evidence and new arguments that bear upon questions of happiness and suffering. Clearly, the chief enemy of open conversation is dogmatism in all its forms… [It] is still granted remarkable scope on questions of both truth and goodness under the banner of religion.[1]

In these few sentences, Sam Harris dismisses the religious contribution to moral reflection. Harris argues that "religion and science are in a zero-sum game with respect to facts" and, therefore, that moral progress depends on us replacing "religious dogmatism" with the fruits of scientific research.[2]

Similar assertions are made by Richard Dawkins[3] and A. C. Grayling, the latter claiming that:

> The foundations of religious belief do not rely upon rationality for their acceptance; so it is not surprising that faith visits violence upon its opponents, for its roots lie in emotion [and]…ignorance… Religion is in fact irrelevant to questions of morality, or it is positively immoral.[4]

The motivations for banishing religious 'dogma' from public moral discourse fall into three main categories. Religion is thought to be **divisive** (as not everyone shares the assumptions from which religious arguments proceed), **reactionary** (religion is supposed to be the last repository of prejudices the wider society has left behind) and **irrational** (religion is said to involve a 'leap of faith' unjustified by reasoned argument).

what this essay will argue

In a range of published and forthcoming essays and reports, Theos has addressed the first two criticisms – responding to the claim that religion is necessarily divisive and reactionary.[5] This essay addresses the third charge against religious reasons. It contends that, far from being uniquely irrational, theism is uniquely capable of explaining why humans can grasp moral reasons at all. It argues that, for 'New Atheists' such as Harris, Dawkins and Grayling, our capacity to transcend the impulses and instincts of natural selection and make moral choices is in the end inexplicable. Ironically, it is these thinkers who are hardest pressed to explain how and why humans can have 'good reason' for their moral and political commitments.

The structure of the argument will be threefold.

Firstly, I will offer a defence of **moral realism** – i.e. that there is a 'truth of the matter' about morality, which our individual moral convictions are trying to get *right*. This is a claim strongly supported by many of the writers most hostile to religion, most notably Sam Harris, along with secular philosophers such as Philippa Foot and Ronald Dworkin.

Secondly, I will argue that **secular worldviews cannot account for our capacity for moral knowledge**. If humans have moral knowledge, it means we have a capacity for getting right things that are not matters of scientific experiment and reasoning alone. On a secular worldview, it is impossible to explain why humans have any capacity (however fallible) for moral knowledge.

> *Only theism can explain why human beings are capable of (fallible) moral knowledge. Theism explains why all of us, theist and atheist alike, are capable of making moral assertions with good reason.*

The third claim of this essay will be that **theism is uniquely able to explain our capacity for moral knowledge**. Harris, Dawkins and Grayling repeatedly claim that religious people have to make moral assertions that lack rational foundations. My argument will be that theism provides the most robust foundations for moral assertions. For only theism can explain why human beings are capable of (fallible) moral knowledge. Theism explains why all of us, theist and atheist alike, are capable of making moral assertions with good reason.

what this essay will *not* argue

The terrain being covered by this essay is ripe for misunderstanding, so it is worth setting out at the start a number of things this essay is not arguing.

It is not arguing that only religious people can be good – or have reason to be good. Many of the reasons for 'doing the right thing' are common to people whether they are religious or not. If the only reason religious people do the right thing is because there is a promise of providential favour now, or an eternal reward in the afterlife, then they are simply equally selfish people with different empirical beliefs. Some of the central religious motivations for actions – love, compassion, duty – are shared by non-religious people. The argument of the essay is that only theism can explain why these moral sentiments correspond to a genuinely objective moral reality. The essay does not argue that only religious people have such motivations, or that only religious people have 'good reason' to act upon them.

It is not arguing that all our moral knowledge comes from religious scriptures or doctrines. The relationship between revelation and reason is an important area of debate and discussion within Christian theology, as it is for many other religions. The argument of this essay allows that even without such revelation we have access to some kind of moral knowledge, and reason to act upon it. This is a view held by a great many – perhaps even most – Christians across the faith's denominations and traditions.

It is not arguing that religious people alone have access to moral truths – or that any one religion has got all moral issues right. To accept 'moral realism' is only to assert that there are right answers to moral questions, not that any individual human being or community has all the right answers *today*. This point is frequently misunderstood – as if to assert that there is a moral reality involves some kind of dogmatism. The very opposite is true: it is because 'moral reality' is objective, because it is not simply constructed out of our preferences and opinions, that it calls us to interrogate our existing views, and continually to be open to the possibility that they may need to be revised.

Finally, it is not arguing against evolution by natural selection or attempting to offer an alternative scientific theory. The argument of the essay accepts and works within the existing scientific consensus. Evolutionary theory is accepted as an account of the way in which human beings have the capacities for reasoning that they do. However, unless the processes of evolution express the purposes of a loving Creator, there is no reason to suppose that the capacity for moral reasoning with which nature endows us will track any kind of objective moral truth.

> *Unless the processes of evolution express the purposes of a loving Creator, there is no reason to suppose that the capacity for moral reasoning with which nature endows us will track any kind of objective moral truth.*

It is inevitable that an essay of this length will leave many readers hungry for rather more detailed philosophical arguments, and feeling that a great deal of territory has been covered very quickly. A fuller treatment of these issues is given in my recently published *From Morality to Metaphysics: The Theistic Implications of our Moral Commitments*.[6] It has a more detailed engagement with the leading contemporary moral philosophers, both realists and anti-realists.[7]

some definitions

Although not written for an academic audience, this essay will use terms that are more common in academic than in popular discourse, and which, therefore, demand brief explanation. Throughout the essay, I will use the term 'moral realism' to denote the conviction that there are objectively right and wrong answers to questions like 'How ought human beings to behave in specified circumstances?' and 'What states of affairs, activities or character traits are valuable and worthy of pursuit?' To a philosopher, this formulation may seem too vague, most notably the meaning of 'objective.' In *From Morality to Metaphysics*, I offer a more technical definition of moral realism, as consisting in the following theses:

(1) The moral order has certain properties, independent of either human beliefs or conceptual schemes. Indeed, the moral order would exist and have properties even if no human beings existed at all; and

(2) A moral judgment is true if and only if it is an adequate representation of the way the moral order is, where 'the world' is as construed in (1).[8]

The essay will argue that when (1) and (2) are combined with the further claim that

(3) Humans have some, albeit fallible, capacity to come to a knowledge of these objective moral truths

this generates a problem for secular worldviews. If human beings have some ability to track a moral order that is *independent* of beliefs, some explanation will need to be given of that harmony between our beliefs and this objective reality – of why our cognitive capacities are (however fallibly) 'truth-tracking'.

the wider context

While this essay engages with philosophical rather than political arguments, the motivations for writing are very practical. It emerges from the *Contending Modernities* research programme at the University of Notre Dame, which is exploring the ways in which different cultures and worldviews build a common life.

The essay is written in the conviction that arguments for the practical utility of religion are necessary, but not sufficient, in making the case for religious public reasoning. It is not enough to show that religious reasons are useful in inspiring social action and engagement with neighbours. It will argue we need to take them seriously as *reasons* as well as motivations. In doing so, it seeks to move the debate about religion and public life beyond a simple dispute about whether 'faith' is useful social glue or a reactionary force which generates division.

This essay has practical implications, namely that religious reasons should be engaged with in the same way as any others offered in the public square. Truth-claims are tested and debated *and* a common life has to be built, peaceably and constructively, while that debate continues to go on. That is the business of politics, which goes on alongside these philosophical debates: to help human beings build a common life, in the midst of this ongoing debate and disagreement.

> *Religious reasons should be engaged with in the same way as any others offered in the public square.*

introduction references

1   Sam Harris, *The Moral Landscape: How Science can Determine Human Values* (London: Swan Books, 2010), p. 39.

2   Ibid., pp. 37-8.

3   Richard Dawkins, *The God Delusion* (New York: Random House, 2006).

4   A. C. Grayling, *The Choice of Hercules: Pleasure, Duty and the Good Life in the 21st Century* (London: Phoenix Books, 2008), pp. 121-22.

5   On the alleged divisiveness of religion, see Nick Spencer, *'Doing God': A Future for Faith in the Public Square* (London: Theos, 2006) and Jonathan Chaplin, *Multiculturalism: A Christian Retrieval* (London: Theos, 2011).

6   Angus Ritchie, *From Morality to Metaphysics: The Theistic Implications of our Moral Commitments* (Oxford University Press, 2012).

7   The key philosophers discussed include John Mackie (anti-realist), Simon Blackburn and Allan Gibbard (quasi-realist), Christine Korsgaard (constructivist), Timothy Scanlon, Philippa Foot (realist) and David Wiggins and John McDowell (who would deliberately resist categorisation as 'realist' or 'anti-realist').

8   Ritchie, *From Morality*, p. 40.

why moral realism?

It was significant that when I came back to Oxford in 1945, that was the time when the news of the concentration camps was coming out. This news was shattering in a fashion that no one now can easily understand… [I]n the face of the news of the concentration camps, I thought 'it just can't be the way [the logical positivists] say it is, that morality in the end is just the expression of an attitude'… [A]ccording to these theories, there is a gap between the facts, or grounds, for a moral judgement and that judgement itself. For whatever reasons might be given for a moral judgement, people might without error refuse to assent to it, not finding the relevant feelings or attitudes in themselves. And this is what I thought was wrong. For, fundamentally, there is no way, if one takes this line, that one could imagine oneself saying to a Nazi, 'but we are right, and you are wrong' with there being any substance to the statement.[1]

In this 2003 interview, Philippa Foot, a leading secular philosopher, identifies the central argument for moral realism. Outside the seminar room, human beings share a deep-seated conviction that the rightness and wrongness of many human actions is in some way objective. One piece of evidence for this is our response to moral outrages such as the concentration camps, and the widespread conviction that their wrongness is not simply a matter of taste or of opinion.

Another piece of evidence that we are all (initially at least) moral realists is the way we reflect on how best to act. When we deliberate on how to act on matters of moral significance, we do more than consult our preferences and tastes. From the inside, at least, it seems as if we are trying to get something *right*. We assume there is some kind of distinction between areas in which our preferences are simply matters of taste, and those in which our preferences are grounded in, and justified by, something deeper. Ronald Dworkin contrasts the attitude we take to statements founded on preference (e.g. our view of the merits of soccer as opposed to, say, rugby) with those where we take our preferences to be justified by some kind of moral reality (e.g. our view on the badness of abortion, or on the badness of preventing free access to abortion):

If someone says that soccer is a 'bad' or 'worthless' game, for example, he may well concede on reflection, that his distaste for soccer is entirely 'subjective' – that he doesn't regard that game as in any 'objective' sense less worthwhile than the game he prefers to watch. Though he has a reason for not watching soccer, he might say, no one whose tastes are different has the same reason.

So when I say that the badness of abortion is objective…it would be natural to understand me as explaining that I do not regard my views about abortion in the same way… The claim that abortion is objectively wrong seems equivalent, that is, in ordinary discourse, to…[the claim] that abortion would still be wrong even if no one thought it was… I mean that abortion is just plain wrong, not wrong only because people think it is.[2]

These remarks of Foot and Dworkin highlight the *prima facie* reasonableness of moral realism. Before we engage in philosophical reflection, human beings are disposed to make a contrast between (a) judgments of mere preference and (b) judgments where we take our preferences to be signs of, and to be accountable to, some more objective standard of truth.[3]

Foot and Dworkin are both 'secular' philosophers, in the sense that neither of them believes in a personal deity, and neither of them seeks to found his or her moral realism on religious arguments. In recent years, the balance of opinion among secular philosophers has moved significantly towards moral realism.[4] Two key factors explain this trend: firstly, a **rejection of reductionist accounts of the universe**, and secondly, the recognition that moral anti-realism has **unacceptable ethical implications**. I will consider each of these factors in turn.

against reductionism

J. L. Mackie's *Ethics: Inventing Right and Wrong* is perhaps the most prominent modern critique of moral realism. Mackie's argument is threefold. Firstly, moral realism involves postulating metaphysically 'problematic' items in the universe (namely, moral truths); secondly, there is no rational basis for our moral beliefs, so, unless we admit they are something like tastes, we are forced to accept that we discover moral truth via our intuitions; and, thirdly, in any case, we do not need moral realism to underwrite our moral convictions.

In this section, I will focus on the first of Mackie's objections – that moral realism involves postulating entities which are somehow metaphysically problematic. Mackie correctly notes that, for the realist, moral truths or imperatives must be both *objective* (that is to say, they exist whether or not we believe in them) and *prescriptive* (that is to say, they have some rational claim over us: when we become aware of them, we ought to obey them).

A decisive way of answering Mackie's worry would be to demonstrate that there are other kinds of statements that have both of these qualities. For then, it cannot be an objection to moral realism that it entails statements that have this same combination of properties.

If scientific enquiry is aimed at truth, we must suppose there to be principles that tell us how to judge rival theories, and to determine what counts as good evidence for what.

If scientific enquiry is aimed at truth, we must suppose there to be principles that tell us how to judge rival theories, and to determine what counts as good evidence for what. The principles by which we judge between theories, and decide what is to count as a 'good explanation' must have the very properties Mackie rejects. That is to say, they must be objective (otherwise science collapses into subjectivism, and becomes a mere matter of opinion) and also prescriptive (they tell us what we *ought* to believe on the basis of the evidence before us).

The philosopher David Enoch offers us an example. A physicist sees a vapour trail in a cloud chamber and infers the presence of a proton. The physicist's hypothesis (or, rather, the complex theory of which it is a small part) is the best scientific explanation for the phenomenon in question. We cannot engage in any serious attempt to make sense of the world around us without principles of Inference to the Best Explanation (IBE). Giving up the attempt to make sense of that world is not a realistic alternative.

> When we choose between rival theories, we rely upon a number of principles of IBE. These principles, by which we interpret empirical evidence, cannot themselves emerge from the process of scientific experimentation. We must have some prior basis for determining what evidence justifies which conclusions.[5]

There is, then, a sense in which all scientific endeavours rely on a certain kind of faith. Not 'faith' in the sense of 'an irrational leap into the dark,' but a belief that these principles by which we sift and weigh evidence are indeed 'truth-tracking'. There is no non-circular way of defending these most basic rational principles. For we have to rely on these principles of reasoning in order to argue for or against anything else.

What should one say to a sceptic who doubts the reliability of our human ways of reasoning? Perhaps she will agree with us that we cannot understand and explain the world without relying upon them, but will then point out we have no independent reason to think the world is explicable. How do we know our best principles of reasoning and inference actually track the truth?

David Enoch offers a convincing *ad hominem* response to the sceptic:

> The explanatory project is intrinsically indispensable because it is one we cannot – and certainly ought not to – fail to engage in, it is unavoidable for we are essentially explanatory creatures. Of course, we can easily refrain from explaining one thing or another, and it's not as if all of us have to be amateur scientists. But we cannot stop explaining altogether, we cannot stop trying to make sense – *some sense* – of what is going on around us.[6]

Enoch's point here, against the philosophical sceptic, is that we have no choice but to try and explain and make sense of the world around us. He wants to draw a parallel between the trust we must give to our rational faculties and the trust we must give to our most basic moral convictions. Just as we cannot stop trying to make sense of the world around us (and thereby seeking scientific explanations), human beings cannot stop trying to work out what is the right thing to do, and what is the best way to live. In the same way as scepticism about our rational faculties is something we can entertain in the seminar room, but not something we can live by, Enoch argues that scepticism about our moral faculties is also something we can debate intellectually, but not something we can seriously live by. This is not to say that we have to take our moral faculties – any more than our other rational ones – to be infallible. They can be improved by reflection and critique, but such reflection and critique itself implies some basic level of trust in our faculties.

A more condensed and pugnacious version of this argument is advanced by Sam Harris, who writes in *The Moral Landscape: How Science can Determine Moral Values*:

> It is essential to see that the demand for radical justification levelled by the moral sceptic could not be met by any branch of science. Science is defined with reference to the goal of understanding the processes at work in the universe. Can we justify this goal scientifically? Of course not. Does this make science itself *unscientific*? If so, we appear to have pulled ourselves *down* by our bootstraps.
>
> It would be impossible to prove that our definition of science is correct, because our standards of proof will be built into any proof we could offer. What evidence could prove that we should value evidence? What logic could demonstrate the importance of logic? ... [N]o-one thinks that this failure of standard science to silence all possible dissent has any significance whatsoever; why should we demand more of a science of morality?[7]

As we shall see, one of Sam Harris' greatest weaknesses is his over-hasty dismissal of alternative positions. This quote is a case in point. Fortunately there are compelling, and more nuanced, arguments for the position he is defending (most obviously, those offered by David Enoch).

the 'New Atheists' and moral realism

The moral realism of many of the 'New Atheists' reflects this change in secular philosophy. In the previous generation, J. L. Mackie was not only the author of one of the most prominent critiques of moral realism, but also of one of the prominent critiques of theism.[8] Many of today's most vocal advocates of atheism are also trenchant in their commitment to the existence of objective moral truths. Sam Harris is the clearest example:

> [T]here are right and wrong answers to moral questions, just as there are right and wrong answers to questions of physics, and such answers may one day fall within reach of the maturing sciences of mind.[9]

This sounds like a fairly straightforward assertion of moral realism, although Harris is at pains to deny that it has any dramatic metaphysical implications. We are told that he is "certainly not claiming that moral truths exist *independent* of the experience of conscious beings," but that "given that there are facts – *real* facts – to be known about how conscious beings can experience the worst possible misery and the greatest possible well-being, it is objectively true to say that there are right and wrong answers to moral questions."[10]

Harris seems to take these "*real* facts" to be prescriptive as well as objective. He gives short shrift to those who would worry about making such an inference from facts about what enables humans to flourish to facts about what is right and wrong:

> The most common objection to my argument is some version of the following: "But you haven't said *why* the well-being of conscious beings *ought* to matter to us. If someone wants to torture all conscious beings to the point of madness, what is to say that he isn't just as 'moral' as you are?"[11]

Harris' response is to deny that "anyone sincerely believes that this kind of moral scepticism makes sense" and to argue that "through reason alone" we can know that "consciousness is the only intelligible domain of value" and hence that making conscious pleasure and pain the basis for human values and morality is "not an arbitrary starting-point".[12]

A. C. Grayling offers a similar account of moral truth. He rejects the 'transcendentalism' of the Judaeo-Christian tradition, on which "man's good lies in submission to an external authority," but he does affirm

> the fundamental idea…that people possess reason, and that by using it they can choose lives worth living for themselves and respectful of their fellows… In humanist ethics the individual is responsible for achieving the good as a free member of a community of free agents [whereas] in religious ethics he achieves the good by obedience to an authority which tells him what his goals are and how he should live.[13]

Grayling takes there to be better and worse answers to the questions of what lives are worth living, and in which ways we ought to be respectful of our fellows. He regards "the arms trade, poverty in the Third World, the continuance of slavery under many guises and names…[and] the ethical challenge posed by environmental problems caused by the heedless and insatiable rush for economic growth everywhere" – as well, of course, as the "antipathies and conflicts" generated by religion – as among the most important and urgent moral issues of our time.[14]

Moral truth is discerned not invented.

On the definition of 'moral realism' being used in this essay, Grayling counts as a moral realist – just as Harris does. Both take the question 'how ought I to live?' to have better or worse answers, which amount to more than statements of what is in my self-interest. On both thinkers' accounts, the truth of the matter is not constituted by our preferences or the conventions of our culture. For both, as for the argument of this essay, moral truth is discerned not invented.

moral anti-realism

The case for moral realism is has both positive and negative components. I have sketched out the positive part: namely, that the way all agents deliberate on how best to act presupposes an objective truth about what are better or worse ways to behave. The negative part of the case is that anti-realism undermines some of our most deeply-held moral convictions.

It is significant that moral anti-realists resist this conclusion; they generally want to argue that these theories leave our ordinary moral practices more or less undisturbed. Most anti-realists would agree with Harris that moral relativism is unacceptable; that the wrongness of torture, slavery and prejudice is culture-transcendent, and we should not be cowed into inaction by the thought that these views are simply 'our' convictions.[15]

They therefore deny that anti-realism has these unacceptable conclusions. Mackie's 'error theory of ethics' is a sophisticated example of this.

morality as invention: Mackie's error theory of ethics

One of Mackie's central contentions is that, once we have recognised the error underlying 'common-sense' morality, and accept that morality is 'made' not 'discovered', most of our moral practice can go on much as before. Indeed, Mackie thinks that accepting that we invent morality has positive practical advantages. Once we realise that moral systems are chosen not discovered, we are in a better position to cast off the more restrictive and prejudiced aspects of our existing moral worldview.

The central weakness of Mackie's position has already been identified. If we accept that morality is something we make and not something we discover, we have no adequate way of distinguishing tastes from convictions. Saying that soccer is a worthless game, and perhaps even preferring a world in which no-one played soccer, is not simply a less intense form of moral preference. It is of a different *order* from the thought that abortion is wrong – or indeed that restricting access to abortion is wrong. What differentiates my preference for a world in which no-one (or everyone) plays soccer from my preference for a world in which no foetus is aborted (or no woman restricted from accessing abortions) is not simply its intensity.

The only adequate way to express the qualitative difference between these sentiments is to use the kind of language deployed by Foot and Dworkin. In the case of abortion, my moral sentiments present themselves as a reaction to something objective, in the way that my tastes, however intense, do not. (This is the same point Foot was making when she discussed her moral revulsion on first hearing the news about the Nazi concentration camps). For this reason, it is not possible to change our metaphysical beliefs without changing our sentiments. Once we come to believe that 'the right attitude to abortion' is chosen, not discovered, and that the wrongness of concentration camps lies in the facts not simply in our judgments, the nature of our moral attitudes is necessarily transformed.

A key area in which 'moral progress' has been made is in an expansion of the circle of our moral concerns to include those whose dignity, rights, and needs have previously been obscured.

As we have seen, Mackie does accept that his error theory will lead to *some* changes in the way we go about moral reflection. He seeks to present his account as one which is more hospitable to progressive social forces than objectivism. One can see why, at first blush, this might seem plausible. There is an obvious conservatism in the arguments Foot, Dworkin and Enoch offer for moral realism, as they are based on a refusal to abandon our most fundamental first-order moral-commitments.

Which social changes should count as 'progressive' is, of course, a moot point. However, if we look at recent history, all the moral philosophers we have considered (realist and anti-realist alike) would agree that a key area in which 'moral progress' has been made is in an expansion of the circle of our moral concerns to include those (humans and perhaps nonhumans) whose dignity, rights, and needs have previously been obscured.

Moral realism is able to make sense of this expansion in our circle of moral concerns – and leaves open the possibility that further extensions may yet be called for. It provides us with a rationale for the constant re-examination of the prevailing moral consensus – and requires us to take seriously the proposal that our individual convictions and communal *status quo* might need revision on behalf of those whom they exclude. This offers the possibility of coming to recognize the claims of those who have previously been thought less than fully human. (The realist must also face the question of moral claims non-humans may or may not have upon us.)

How one determines the moral significance and claims of different agents is itself a complex question. But precisely because it conceives of ethics as a matter of discovery rather than invention, moral realism permits a conception of progress through an increasing openness to the lives and insights of others. By contrast, any account of morality which understands it to be 'made' rather than 'discovered' will be unable to give any serious, non-circular content to the idea that we might 'make' our morality in a 'better' way – where 'better' is analysed as giving a due regard to the interests of beings we have previously oppressed or ignored.

conclusion

This chapter has advanced both a positive and a negative case for moral realism. The positive case is that realism is (in Enoch's words) "deliberatively indispensable". We can, of course, conceive of the possibility that moral truth is constituted by our sentiments or cultural conventions, but every time we reflect on how best to act in a situation, the very process of deliberation implies we are trying to get something right. The negative case against anti-realism is twofold: its principal objections to realism do not hold water, and its proponents fail to face up to the extent to which it will indeed undermine moral practice.

In the following chapter, I will argue that secular moral realists are unable to explain human knowledge of this reality. This is one reason why some secular philosophers shy away from moral realism. Unlike Sam Harris, they recognise that moral realism may lead on to a wider metaphysic that sits uneasily with an atheistic worldview. This may account for the work being done in secular philosophy on intermediate positions between anti-realism and realism. Examples include John McDowell's 'anti-anti-realism,' Christine Korsgaard's 'procedural realism' and Simon Blackburn's 'quasi-realism'.[16]

If this critique of secular moral philosophy is justified, we are left in an intriguing position. The cry of the 'New Atheists' is that religious reasons ought to be kept out of public reasoning because they are uniquely irrational. The argument of this essay, and the more detailed case made in *From Morality to Metaphysics*, is that the very opposite is true. For only theism is able to explain why we can have confidence in our faculties for reasoning about how we ought to act.

chapter 1 – references

1   Alex Voorhoeve, 'The Grammar of Goodness: An Interview with Philippa Foot', *Harvard Review of Philosophy* 11 (2003), pp. 33-34.

2   Ronald Dworkin, 'Objectivity and Truth: You'd Better Believe It', *Philosophy and Public Affairs* 25(2) (1996), p. 98.

3   Some philosophers would wish to categorise statements about aesthetics as purely matters of taste, whilst others would argue that aesthetic judgments are also accountable to some kind of objective standards. That debate falls outside the scope of this report. Here, our concern will be about whether there is some kind of objective standard to which our moral judgments are accountable.

4   These include Geoffrey Sayre-McCord (see his edited collection *Essays on Moral Realism*, published by Cornell University Press in 1988); Timothy Scanlon (whose 2009 Locke Lectures in Oxford mark a shift to a strong moral realism) and John McDowell (whose position might more fairly be called 'anti-anti-realism', but who is clear that moral statements have as much of a title to 'truth' as scientific ones – see his 'Two Sorts of Naturalism' in his *Mind, Value and Reality* (Cambridge, MA: Harvard University Press, 1998)).

5   David Enoch, 'An Outline of an Argument for Robust Metanormative Realism', in Russ Shafer-Landau (ed.), *Oxford Studies in Metaethics*, vol. II (Oxford: Oxford University Press, 2007), pp. 21-50.

6   Ibid., pp. 33-4.

7   Harris, *Moral Landscape*, op. cit., p. 56.

8   J. L. Mackie, *The Miracle of Theism: Arguments For and Against the Existence of God* (Oxford: Oxford University Press, 1982).

9   Harris, *Moral Landscape*, p. 43

10   Ibid., p. 44. Italics in original text.

11   Ibid., p. 49.

12   Ibid., pp. 49-50.

13   A. C. Grayling, *What is good? Searching for the best way to live* (London: Phoenix, 2003).

14   Grayling, *The Choice of Hercules*, op. cit., pp. 64-5.

15   For an excellent exposure of the self-refuting nature of a moral relativism founded on respect for other cultures, see Terry Eagleton, *The Illusions of Postmodernism* (London: Wiley-Blackwell, 1996). Charles Taylor argues that genuine respect for other cultures in fact requires the possibility of substantive disagreement in his *Multiculturalism and the 'Politics of Recognition'* (Princeton: Princeton University Press, 1994).

16   Cf. John McDowell, *Mind, Value and Reality* (Cambridge, MA: Harvard University Press, 1998); Christine Korsgaard, *The Sources of Normativity*, ed. Onora O'Neill with responses by G. A. Cohen, Raymond Geuss, Thomas Nagel, and Bernard Williams (Cambridge: Cambridge University Press, 1996); Simon Blackburn, *Ruling Passions* (Oxford: Oxford University Press, 1998). *From Morality*

to Metaphysics offers a detailed exposition and evaluation of these positions. It argues that each theory fails, and that the failure is systemic. The less realist positions (such as Blackburn's and Korsgaard's) are ultimately unable to underwrite our most fundamental ethical commitments. Such theories deny the existence of an independent moral order. Instead, they take it to be constituted either by our sentiments or conventions. Despite much skilful philosophical footwork, they are unable to avoid undermining our practices of moral deliberation, and our motivations for moral action. By contrast, the more realist theories cannot provide either an adequate explanation of our capacity for moral knowledge – nor (as McDowell claims) can they reject the demand for such an explanation as somehow unjustified.

2

science and moral knowledge

The previous chapter presented the case for moral realism – a case whose general outline many of the 'New Atheists' would accept. This chapter will move the argument on by positing that atheists are unable to explain the human capacity for moral knowledge, thereby seriously undermining the polemic of writers such as Harris and Dawkins.

what kind of explanation is needed?

When we consider the human capacity for knowledge, three sets of questions need to be asked. They often get confused, and so it is important to distinguish them with some care. The first question asks for the *justification* of our beliefs, the second asks for a *historical explanation* of why humans have come to the kinds of views they have, and the third asks for a *causal explanation* of why humans' cognitive capacities have one particular property, in this case that of (however fallibly) tracking the truth.

There is no non-circular way of justifying our trust in the reliability of our most basic cognitive capacities.

The first question was addressed by David Enoch's arguments. As we saw in our earlier discussion, human beings cannot avoid having a certain kind of faith in their rational faculties. There is no non-circular way of justifying our trust in the reliability of our most basic cognitive capacities. We can propose incremental changes to the ways in which we reason; to the way we choose one explanation rather than another on the basis of evidence, or the way we decide one course of action is (pragmatically or morally) better than another, but that process of incremental change always has to be done on the basis of reasons.

We can never hope to construct a holistic justification for our trust in the human capacity to reason, and it is an important insight of modern philosophy (which has moved in recent years away from both anti-realism and the search for sceptic-proof foundations for knowledge) that no such holistic justification is needed. Global scepticism, whether about scientific explanation or about moral reasoning, is not a position human beings can live by even if they are able to entertain it in the seminar room. It is legitimate to proceed, and only possible to proceed, by taking our capacity for moral and theoretical reasoning to be at least partially capable of tracking the truth.

What of the second and third questions, pertaining to historical and causal explanations? I will argue below that, in the case of our capacity for scientific knowledge, an atheistic understanding of evolution by natural selection looks as if it can answer *both* the historical question (of how our cognitive capacities have arisen) *and* the causal question (of how these capacities come to be truth-tracking). However, it is far harder to see how an atheistic understanding of natural selection can explain why our capacities for moral reflection are capable of tracking the truth.

evolution and human cognition

Richard Dawkins' 1995 article 'Where D'you Get Those Peepers?' popularises work done by evolutionary scientists on the development of the human eye.[1] Assuming a process of purely random mutations among the precursors of human beings, and the survival of those precursors with mutations that enhance the animal's capacity for survival and replication, these scientists have shown why something as complex and sensitive to the external environment as the human eye might have been expected to develop.

While there is ongoing debate among scientists on some of the details of evolutionary theory,[2] its broad outlines are plausible and compelling. Evolution by natural selection looks capable of explaining why humans would develop beliefs about the physical objects around them which tracked the objective external reality, through the account it gives of the emergence of physical organs such as the eye that are sensitive to that reality.

In the same way, natural selection looks well-suited to explaining how humans have developed truth-tracking capacities for theoretical reasoning, such as choosing between competing scientific theories, or evaluating philosophical arguments. It seems plausible to claim that those of our ancestors whose cognitive faculties tracked the truth would have a significant evolutionary advantage over those whose did not. Among competing groups of humans (and their evolutionary precursors) truth-tracking capacities for theoretical reasoning would be beneficial to the survival and flourishing of the collective.

For both our knowledge of our physical surroundings and our capacity for theoretical reasoning, natural selection looks capable of answering all three of the questions we asked at the start of this section, namely, why we are *justified* in trusting our faculties, how they emerged *historically,* and what *causal* story explains why the faculties also track an objective reality.

evolution and moral knowledge

Might the same kind of explanation be on offer for our knowledge of moral truths? At first glance, it looks like a much more difficult case. Whereas there is an obvious relationship between survival value and truth in the case of our perceptual beliefs and our basic capacities for reasoning, it is harder to see why survival value and truth would be connected in the case of our moral beliefs.

Instead of the evolutionary process directly tracking the rightness of moral beliefs, might it not be that survival value and objective rightness are both correlated with some third property? Perhaps moral codes evolve to encourage us to co-operate, and thus to promote collective well-being more effectively. There is both an obvious selective advantage to this and a strong case for thinking the fruits of such co-operation are objectively good. Something like this view is implicit in *The Moral Landscape*. As we have already seen, Sam Harris thinks it is self-evident that human "well-being" is objectively valuable. Indeed, he argues that well-being is the only genuine moral value, all other candidates being relics of religion or other forms of superstition.

Harris' view looks the most plausible way of reconciling the objectivity of morality with the need to explain how humans, as products of the process of natural selection, might come to be able to grasp moral truths. For this reason, the next section will be devoted to a detailed examination of his position.

Sam Harris on science and morality

Harris begins by appealing to our most fundamental moral intuitions. He argues that a moment's reflection will reveal that the only genuinely important moral imperatives relate to the well-being of conscious agents:

Grounding our values in a continuum of conscious states – one that has *the worst possible misery for everyone* at its depths and differing degrees of well-being at all other points – seems like the only legitimate context in which to conceive of values and moral norms. Of course, anyone who has an alternative set of moral axioms is free to put them forward, just as they are free to define 'science' in any way they want. But some definitions will be useless, or worse – and many current definitions of 'morality' are so bad that we can know, far in advance of any breakthrough in the sciences of mind, that they have no place in any serious conversation about how we should live in this world.[3]

A modest version of Harris' claim here seems quite plausible, but rather banal – namely, that 'misery' is at one end of a moral spectrum and happiness and the development of human capacities at another. It is hard to imagine anyone denying this, even the religious thinkers he attacks at considerable length. Mainstream Christian, Jewish and Islamic views all take God to have a fundamental concern for human well-being, and a desire that humans enjoy his compassion and blessing eternally.

Disagreement with Harris will come, not on the value of 'well-being' and the evils of 'misery' but on the questions of (i) how in fact misery is to be minimised and well-being maximised, (ii) what "well-being" actually consists of, and (iii) whether the value of well-being and the disvalue of misery are the *only* moral values. Clearly, the answers to these questions will be different if one thinks the world has been created by a loving God, and that humanity's highest good consists in eternal union with him (as in Christian orthodoxy). In *The Moral Landscape,* Harris offers no arguments that address this issue. Rather, he simply makes the obvious point that *if* the arguments against religion that he has advanced elsewhere are correct, *then* religion has no contribution to make to our discernment of objective moral values.

> *Sam Harris argues that well-being is the only genuine moral value.*

Harris has a tendency to write as if religious thinkers are the main opponents of the position he is advancing (roughly speaking, a moral realism which sees the promotion of positive states of consciousness as the sole moral value). In fact, the most influential secular moral philosophers, including those who are moral realists, would reject his account. For, once we have accepted that 'well being' is valuable and 'misery' is evil (and have further accepted that there is some connection between 'well being' and both physical pleasure and biological flourishing) we have hardly begun to scratch the surface of moral debate. A whole range of questions remain; questions which have preoccupied and perplexed secular philosophers as well as religious ones.

Harris offers the following reasons for believing science will be able to answer the key questions in moral philosophy:

> We will increasingly understand good and evil, right and wrong, in scientific terms, because moral concerns translate into facts about how our thoughts and behaviours affect the well-being of conscious creatures like ourselves. Students of philosophy will notice that this commits me to some kind of moral realism…and some form of consequentialism (viz. the rightness of an act depends on how it impacts on the well-being of conscious creatures.) While moral realism and consequentialism have both come under pressure in philosophical circles, they have the advantage of corresponding to many of our intuitions about how the world works.[4]

The paragraph just quoted involves two striking *non sequiturs*. Firstly, Harris assumes that if we accept his claim that "moral concerns translate into facts about how our thoughts and behaviours affect the well-being of conscious creatures," then we are committed to consequentialism. Secondly, he assumes that the sole metric for the "well-being of conscious creatures like ourselves" must be positive states of experience. In fact, there are extremely powerful arguments against *both* consequentialism and an excessive focus on states of experience – arguments which have been developed by secular philosophers and so do not involve any religious claims.

the value of reality over experience

Why should we assume that the only morally significant value is the impact of actions on our conscious states of experience? Harris offers the following argument:

Without potential consequences at the level of experience...all talk of value is empty. Therefore, to say that an act is morally necessary, or evil, or blameless, is to make (tacit) claims about its consequences in the lives of conscious creatures (whether actual or potential). I am unaware of any interesting exception to this rule.[5]

In his 1974 book *Anarchy, State and Utopia*, Robert Nozick developed a famous and devastating argument against taking conscious experience to be the sole moral value. He invited his readers to consider whether they would value a life in which all human beings were plugged into an 'experience machine' offering maximally pleasurable states of consciousness.[6] His view (confirmed by every group which I have invited to consider the scenario) is that nearly every one of us would decline to be plugged into such a machine.

> *Human beings value things other than positive conscious states. We do not simply want life to be a succession of maximally positive experiences.*

The universally negative response to the offer of an 'experience machine' demonstrates that human beings value things other than positive conscious states. We do not simply want life to be a succession of maximally positive experiences. Human beings want their lives to be, in some wider sense, meaningful. It seems that we value being in authentic contact and fellowship with other people and living lives that in some sense add value to the world around us, such as by exercising artistic and intellectual creativity, caring for other human beings, or undertaking work that is vocational rather than simply remunerative.

As Harris' case for the moral value of 'well-being' is based on an appeal to our most powerful intuitions, he cannot simply dismiss Nozick's appeal to an equally powerful and widely-shared intuition. Yet, if he accepts the validity of this thought-experiment, his entire project is in jeopardy. What Nozick's thought-experiment demonstrates is that human beings have a concern for *what is actually going on in the external world* in a way that is not solely tied to *what human beings experience* and what goes on in their conscious lives. That is to say, they reject any moral theory that locates value entirely in conscious experience.

moral constraints on pursuing positive consequences

Harris' other central claim is that the moral value of actions lies solely in their consequences. Harris tells us he is a consequentialist, distinguishing his moral theory from accounts (such as virtue ethics or deontological views) which impose side-constraints on the maximisation of 'well-being' (however defined).[7] Advocates of virtue ethics or deontology assert (against consequentialism) that some actions are intrinsically wrong and should not be undertaken even if they increase the overall well-being of sentient creatures.[8]

Again, most people's moral intuitions can be shown to run against Harris' position. Philip Kitcher invites us to consider the following scenario:

> Imagine a stereotypical post-holocaust situation in which the survival of the human gene pool depends on copulation between two people. Suppose, for whatever reason, that one of the parties is unwilling to copulate with the other ... Under these circumstances, [the principle of maximizing the survival of the collective] requires the willing person to coerce the unwilling person, using whatever extremes of force are necessary – perhaps even allowing for the murder of those who attempt to defend the reluctant one.[9]

While Kitcher's specific example may seem outlandish, it has been chosen to illuminate a dilemma which we encounter in a less extreme form on a regular basis. A great deal of moral deliberation concerns situations where overall well-being may be enhanced by a course of action from which we nonetheless recoil as intrinsically wrong. Most of us do not take the ends to justify the means – hence, for example, the resistance to the use of torture in counter-terrorism operations.

Harris might object that the wrongness of these acts still lies in their negative consequences for specific conscious agents. (In Kitcher's example, one agent faces being coerced into sexual intercourse and others may be killed.) But being a 'consequentialist' involves far more than weighing acts in terms of their consequences for human agents. It involves the willingness to aggregate well-being. This leaves the consequentialist unable to rule out *any* way of treating other human beings. Given sufficiently large collective benefits, any amount of harm can be justified.

Harris is explicitly committed to aggregating well-being in exactly this way. In a revealing footnote, he considers another thought-experiment of Robert Nozick's. This concerns the possibility of "utility monsters" who gain such enormous satisfaction from devouring human beings that this outweighs the satisfaction lost in those prematurely ended human lives.[10] Harris wonders: Would it be ethical for our species to be "sacrificed for the unimaginably vast happiness of some superbeings"? His response is characteristically blunt:

> Provided that we take the time to really imagine the details (which is not easy), I think the answer is clearly 'yes'. There seems no reason to suppose that we must occupy the highest peak on the moral landscape. If there are beings who stand in relation to us as we do to bacteria, it should be easy to admit that their interests must trump our own, and to a degree that we cannot possibly conceive.[11]

Harris is sanguine about the implications of this answer. After all, he observes, "there is no compelling reason to believe that such superbeings exist, much less ones that want to eat us."[12]

In fact, Harris' response is far more revealing – and damaging – than he seems to imagine. Philosophers such as Nozick and Kitcher are not simply playing games when they present their outlandish thought-experiments. Such thought-experiments are designed to tease out what we take to be of fundamental value and why. And Harris' response to this thought-experiment is, in fact, rather chilling. It reveals that, for him, human beings have no specific and intrinsic dignity. If there is sufficient utility to be gained from their destruction and consumption, then we can imagine situations where that would be perfectly acceptable. Harris' consequentialism undercuts any conception of humans as bearers of inalienable dignity or inviolable rights.

Harris claimed that one of the advantages of consequentialism was that it "correspond[s] to many of our intuitions about how the world works." We can now see that this is manifestly wrong. In reality, it takes a couple of our core moral intuitions (namely, that states of consciousness matter and that the moral significance of actions depends in a significant part on their consequences) and uses them to ride roughshod over other, equally central intuitions. There is no *rational* basis for doing this. Harris supplies no arguments for trusting the moral intuitions he appeals to any more than those he completely ignores. As we have seen, a considerable part of his argument relies on eliding very plausible claims (namely, that conscious states and consequences are of huge moral significance) with much more extreme positions which do not follow from them, namely that *nothing else is of value* than the production of positive conscious states, and that there are no side constraints on what can be justified to promote such states. This is why so few secular philosophers, let alone religious ones, agree with his account.

other secular accounts

There are two reasons for devoting such a significant portion of this essay to Sam Harris' work. Firstly, the popularity of *The Moral Landscape* gives credence to a moral outlook with deeply inhumane implications. For example, Harris' work has been endorsed in glowing terms by the most prominent of the 'New Atheists', Richard Dawkins: "I was one of those who had unthinkingly bought into the hectoring myth that science can say nothing about morals. To my surprise, *The Moral Landscape* has changed all that for me."

Dawkins' words, like several other high-profile endorsements of *The Moral Landscape*, give the impression that Harris' arguments are somehow ground-breaking and progressive.[13] In fact, Harris' position has definite echoes of the 1970s, and another high-profile attempt to found morality on science alone. E. O. Wilson's *Sociobiology: A New Synthesis* provoked a vitriolic response from secular as well as religious writers because he too failed to make an adequate distinction between facts and values (in his case, between what maximizes a species' replication and what is morally right).[14] It appeared that, in calling for a morality based on evolutionary imperatives, Wilson was advocating a moral position which would abandon the weak and vulnerable. He was, in fact, horrified by this interpretation of his views, but all his opponents were doing was pushing his arguments to their logical conclusion. The history of the twentieth century is one that made them rightly wary of the attempt in the name of 'science' and 'progress' to 'tidy up' our moral intuitions and to 'think the unthinkable'.

Wilson's naive equation of biological and moral imperatives is, of course, different from Harris' equation of moral value with the aggregated pleasure and lack of pain experienced by sentient beings. But the structural flaw in the arguments is the same. What Harris and Wilson have in common is a cavalier attitude to the core moral commitments of most human beings and a disregard for centuries of painstaking debate in (secular as well as religious) moral philosophy. This leads them to develop accounts of ethics with deeply unappealing implications, which neither of them seems to have thought through. In consequence, their accounts of the foundations of morality need to be vigorously contested, for their widespread acceptance would have consequences for public policy which should be of grave concern to atheists and theists alike. This is not (as Harris and Dawkins would like to claim) an issue *between* religious and secular thought. The great irony for the 'New Atheists' is that *The Moral Landscape* does no justice to the richness and nuance of secular moral philosophy.

The second reason for examining Harris' argument at such length is that it is one of the few that looks capable of explaining how humans come to possess truth-tracking moral faculties. If moral judgment were as closely tied to scientific knowledge as Harris (or indeed E. O. Wilson) suggests, it would not be hard to explain why our moral faculties track the truth – for we already have an explanation for the way our capacities for theoretical reasoning track the truth, and (on Harris and Wilson's accounts) moral reasoning is more or less a subset of empirical science. If, however, moral reasoning is a more complex and distinctive subject-matter, it becomes very difficult to explain how human beings have developed the distinct cognitive capacities that enable them to discern moral truths.

Unless we fall back into seeing morality as a matter of invention (which is unsatisfactory for the reasons already given), the question arises of how we make the *right* choices in developing a moral code that goes beyond the imperatives of gene-, organism-, or species-replication. Richard Dawkins seeks to answer this question in *The God Delusion* (written before *The Moral Landscape* was published). Dawkins suggests that we can "pull ourselves up by our bootstraps" now that humans have developed to a stage where we can reflect on the biological imperatives we have inherited. We can choose to act in ways that protect the weak and vulnerable, and to create communities which are not governed purely by the survival of the fittest.[15]

> There is going to be no evolutionary explanation available for that part of our moral cognition which does not maximise the survival and replication of the species.

This seems an accurate account of what goes on when we reason morally, but it fails to explain how we have the capacity for accurate moral reasoning. When we seek to 'pull ourselves up by our bootstraps', we take ourselves to have the capacity to discern what is morally better or worse. Natural selection can offer no account of why our moral intuitions and sentiments (insofar as they take us beyond the bare imperatives of survival and replication) should track an objective truth. There is going to be no evolutionary explanation available for that part of our moral cognition which does not maximise the survival and replication of the species. Yet, by Dawkins' own reckoning, it is that part of our moral cognition that enables us to make the most important ethical advances – to have compassion and care for the weak.

conclusion

From the arguments offered In this chapter, it seems that secular accounts of morality face an impossible task. For they need *both* to be sufficiently realist to do justice to our most fundamental moral commitments *and* to be able to explain why our processes of moral reflection are capable of tracking this objective moral order. Nothing offered by the 'New Atheists' comes anywhere close to meeting the challenge – and (as I indicated at the end of the previous chapter) the same problem faces even the most nuanced of secular moral philosophers.

What requires explanation is the surprising harmony between (i) the objective moral order (which, as I argued in Chapter One, we have reason to believe exists) and (ii) the cognitive capacities of human beings. It is a harmony deeply suggestive of design – for the actions of a purposive agent would explain the correlation between human capacities and the objective moral order. To writers such as Dawkins and Harris, the promise of natural selection is that it can explain such harmonies *without* invoking such an agent. Natural selection explains why some processes are goal-directed without requiring the goals to be goals of any particular agent. When it comes to knowledge of the external world, for example, or basic processes of logical inference, there is a definite selective advantage to having a cognitive apparatus that gets things (objectively) right.

What is morally right is not always what is conducive to maximising the survival and replication of one's own particular group.

However, when it comes to morality, there is no such advantage. As Dawkins concedes, what is morally right is *not* always what is conducive to maximising the survival and replication of one's own particular group – or indeed the human race as a whole. To say this is not to cast doubt on natural selection as a mode of scientific explanation. This essay is not offering an argument against the theory of evolution, but rather builds on work Theos has already done on the compatibility of this theory with theism.[16]

What is clear from the argument of this chapter is that selective advantage cannot explain our capacity for discerning (however fallibly) the moral truth. This is not a temporary gap in scientific knowledge. We have shown that *in principle*, an atheistic construal of natural selection cannot provide an explanation for our capacity for moral knowledge. Atheistic versions of natural selection can explain why humans will have some capacity for co-operation and mutual sympathy, as these will obviously enhance the species' survival and replication rates. But, as we have argued, there is sometimes a definite divergence – between what maximises species survival and replication and what we have reason to believe is morally right. Whether our moral faculties are as they are because of their survival value or because they are mere accidental epiphenomena of evolution, the same problem arises. In either case, the atheist lacks an explanation for the fact that these faculties are (however fallibly) capable of discerning an objective moral order. In the next chapter, I will argue that natural selection can account for the reliability of our faculties only when it is understood theistically – that is, as the means by which God creates a world with intelligent beings who have a capacity for knowledge of goodness and for loving relationships.

chapter 2 references

1   Richard Dawkins, 'Where D'you Get Those Peepers?', *New Statesman and Society*, 16 June 1995, p. 29 and Dan-Erik Nilsson and Susanne Pelger, 'A Pessimistic Estimate of the Time Required for an Eye to Evolve', *Proceedings of the Royal Society of London*, Biological Sciences 256 (1994), pp. 53–8.

2   See S. J. Gould and R. C. Lewontin, 'The Spandrels of San Marco and the Panglossian Paradigm: A Critique Of The Adaptationist Programme', *Proceedings of The Royal Society of London*, Series B, 205(1161) (1979) pp. 581-98; more recently, see Richard Dawkins, 'The descent of Edward Wilson', *Prospect*, May 2012, and the ensuing vigorous correspondence concerning Wilson's book, *The Social Conquest of Earth*, in that magazine and elsewhere.

3   Harris, *Moral Landscape*, op. cit., p. 61.

4   Ibid.

5   Ibid., pp. 85-6.

6   Robert Nozick, *Anarchy, State, and Utopia*. (New York: Basic Books, 1974), pp. 42-45.

7   Virtue ethics emphasises the 'virtues' or 'character' of the moral agent in question, asking what kind of person s/he should be. Deontological ethics emphasises the rules that the moral agent should follow, asking what actions are prohibited, permitted or mandatory.

8   Consequentialism argues that the rightness or wrongness of a moral act is dependent only on the consequences of that act.

9   Philip Kitcher, 'Four Ways of "Biologicizing" Ethics', in *Mendel's Mirror: Philosophical Reflections on Biology* (Oxford: Oxford University Press, 2003), p. 328.

10   Nozick, *Anarchy*, p. 14.

11   Harris, *Moral Landscape*, p. 271.

12   Ibid.

13   Dawkins' endorsement, along with endorsements from Ian McEwan and Stephen Pinker, appears on the cover of *The Moral Landscape*, and online at http://www.samharris.org/the-moral-landscape (accessed 10 September 2012).

14   E. O. Wilson, *Sociobiology: The New Synthesis* (Cambridge, MA: Harvard University Press, 1975). See also my discussion of the controversy in Ritchie, *From Morality*, pp. 57ff., and Ullica Segerstråle, *Defenders of the Truth: The Sociobiology Debate* (Oxford: Oxford University Press, 2000).

15   Dawkins, *God Delusion*, p. 222.

16   Cf. Nick Spencer and Denis Alexander, *Rescuing Darwin* (London: Theos, 2009)

from goodness to God

This essay has argued that humans have to trust our cognitive capacities. In particular, it has argued that we have to trust our moral faculties. It has further claimed that atheists lack any convincing account of why our moral faculties track a truth which is independent of our sentiments and cultural conventions. This chapter argues that, by contrast, theism can explain this harmony between our moral faculties and an objective moral order.

theism and the theory of evolution

To argue that theism can explain the harmony between our moral faculties and the objective moral order is not to set it up as a competitor to evolutionary biology. The relationship between theism and evolutionary biology is analogous to the relationship between theism and fundamental physics. The existence of a benevolent God is held by many theists to explain the fact the universe appears to be 'fine tuned' to an extraordinary extent, in a way that is hospitable to conscious life.[1] In making this claim, theists are not offering their position as a rival to physics. Indeed, it is physics that has revealed how finely tuned the universe actually is, and how even tiny changes in some of the most fundamental features of the world would make it wholly inhospitable to any conscious life at all.

In the same way, the theistic explanation is intended to complement that offered by evolutionary biology. In neither area is there any suggestion that the scientific theories are wrong, rather that they leave certain characteristics of the world unexplained. These unexplained characteristics are not simply gaps in current knowledge that might be filled in by future scientific progress. With respect to both the 'fine tuning' of the universe, and the human capacity for moral knowledge, the argument made by theists is that *in principle* science is not suited to offering the explanation we need.

explaining moral knowledge

In Chapter 2, we identified three different questions that might be asked of any of our beliefs. The first question asks for the *justification* of those beliefs, the second asks for a *historical explanation* of why humans have come to the kinds of views they have, and the third asks for a *causal explanation* of why humans' cognitive capacities have one particular property, in this case that of (however fallibly) tracking the truth.

This essay does not doubt that evolutionary biology provides a historical explanation of the development of human beings' moral faculties. However, as Chapter Two argued, we have good reason to believe that our moral faculties have the property of *tracking the truth*. It is *this* property of our moral faculties which atheistic versions of evolutionary biology cannot explain. In this chapter, we will consider how classical theism explains this property, and whether it is the only possible explanation.

Philosophers of science have identified two broad categories of explanation. One form of explanation focuses on *laws*. An event is accounted for by showing that it follows logically from the previous state of the world and what we know to be the laws of nature.[2] Another form of explanation focuses on *ends*. We explain something by showing that a system tends towards a certain end-state, and that an event has happened because it is the best way to achieve that particular end. This latter form of explanation is often called a *teleological* explanation (*telos* being the Greek word for 'end').[3]

Evolutionary biology is a form of teleological explanation. It shows why something has happened in terms of the end that is being realised (namely, the survival and replication of the species). It also shows us the mechanism by which the end is realised (namely, random mutations and selective pressure).

We use another kind of teleological explanation every time we account for a piece of intentional human behaviour. An event (e.g. my purchase of a suit) is explained by the fact I desire a particular end-state (e.g. getting a new job), and that I believe a certain set of actions need to be taken in order to achieve that (among them, actions which improve my appearance and so impress the interview panel).

There is much debate among philosophers as to how this kind of explanation fits in with the explanations offered by the physical sciences. The most reductionist philosophers, such as Paul and Patricia Churchland, argue that *all* human actions are ultimately explained by the laws of physics. On their account, humans may have the illusion our actions are expressions of 'purpose' or 'decision', but these terms are simply pieces of 'folk psychology'. These terms can be replaced in the ultimate story by a description of the underlying physical and chemical mechanisms which govern our bodies, including our brains.[4]

While reductionists hold that human behaviour is ultimately explained by physical laws *rather than* by a teleological explanation, they have not shown that an explanation in terms of beliefs and intentions is intrinsically defective. Even a reductionist need not claim that the following chain of statements is *a bad form of explanation* – simply that it is not in fact the ultimate explanation for human behaviour:

(1) An agent had reason to value a state of affairs

therefore

(2) The agent wanted to bring about that state of affairs.

(2), taken together with

(3) The agent believed that doing *X* was the best way to bring about that state of affairs

and

(4) The agent had the power to do *X*

explains why

(5) The agent did *X*

which explains, given (3), how the state of affairs came about.

Statements (1) to (5) clearly constitute a valid explanation of a state of affairs. The claim made by classical theism is that this is the form of explanation we should use to account for the existence and character of the world. As I have stressed already, it is not a form of explanation which seeks to compete with evolutionary biology or the physical sciences.

When theism explains why our moral faculties are reliable, it takes the phenomena described by the sciences – i.e. the initial conditions of the universe, the fundamental laws of physics, and the chemical and biological processes by which life, consciousness and the capacity for rational thought emerge – to be the means by which a loving God has chosen to achieve his purposes.

We might say that such explanations are a 'level up' from the scientific ones. It accounts for features of the world which atheists must regard as vast coincidences. The atheist cannot explain why either (i) the fundamental physical constants in the universe are within the small range that would sustain life or (ii) the moral faculties generated by the combination of initial conditions, mutations and selective pressures are such as to enable us to discern the moral truth. By contrast, theism seeks to explain these phenomena by maintaining that the universe is created and sustained by a good and loving God.

We can test the validity and comprehensiveness of this theistic account against our model of intentional explanation (that is, the numbered statements (1) to (5) above).

Classical theism can explain *why* God values a world in which human beings have moral beliefs that are truth-tracking. God clearly has reason to value that state of affairs, because it is objectively good and (given that God is perfectly good and loving) this explains why God actually values it. (This corresponds with statements (1) and (2) in the model form of explanation.)

According to classical theism, God is both all-powerful and all-knowing. In consequence, God not only has reason to ensure human beliefs are truth-tracking, but has the capacity to create and sustain a universe in which humans evolve with these properties. This corresponds with statements (3) and (4) in the model form of explanation – and so accounts for the way in which the processes of evolution have generated creatures capable of knowing what is objectively good and valuable.[5]

alternatives to classical theism

The fact that classical theism would explain our moral knowledge does not make it true. On the one hand, classical theism is not the only account that can explain our moral knowledge. On the other, an atheist may argue that there are other reasons to reject the position. I will consider these issues in turn.

Firstly, it is certainly true that classical theism is not the only possible teleological explanation. Some faiths hold that the universe reflects the purposes of a variety of divine agents, while a small number of contemporary philosophers have argued for a quasi-Platonic view on which goodness itself is creative.[6] (Indeed, one proponent of this view calls it an 'abstract conception of God').[7] I have explained elsewhere why, as a Christian philosopher, I take classical theism to be the most powerful and satisfying of these various teleological explanations.[8] The scope of this essay is more limited, as it is an argument to the effect that that *theism* makes sense of our moral commitments in a way that atheism cannot. Questions as to the merits of different religious worldviews are of course very important, but are distinct from this argument. What this essay has sought to show is that in order to account for humans' moral knowledge, it is necessary to understand the nature of the world as expressing a benevolent purpose.[9]

Turning to the second point, it is certainly possible to accept the argument of this essay, and yet to remain staunchly atheist. One might agree that atheism leaves our moral faculties unexplained, and yet hold that there are other more powerful reasons for rejecting theism (for example, that theism is internally incoherent, or that it is unable to explain the existence and extent of suffering in the universe). In consequence, the argument being made in this essay is only one part of an intellectual case for theism.[10] However, the purpose of this essay (as outlined in the Introduction) has not been to offer a decisive apologetic argument for theism but rather to advance some serious reasons for considering the truth-claims, as well as the utility, of religious faith.

conclusion

As indicated in the introduction, there are a number of things this essay has *not* been trying to do. It has not argued that only religious people can be good (or have reason to be good), nor that all our moral knowledge comes from religious scriptures or doctrines. It has not argued that only religious people have access to moral truths, nor has it sought to contradict, or offer an alternative to, evolutionary biology. Nor, indeed, has the essay sought to offer a knock-down argument for theism in general, let alone for Christianity in particular. Rather, it has advanced a much more limited claim, but one that still has significant implications for the way we treat religious reasons in the public square.

In the area of morality, unlike many other kinds of knowledge, truth and selective advantage look to be very different things. On an atheistic worldview, it seems impossible to explain why the two converge.

In this essay I have argued that only religious worldviews can explain why humans have moral knowledge. It is one thing to explain why moral conventions of a certain kind develop, as they assist the replication and multiplication of a group. It is quite another to explain why humans should develop a capacity to discern moral *truth*. In the area of morality, unlike many other kinds of knowledge, truth and selective advantage look to be very different things. On an atheistic worldview, it seems impossible to explain why the two converge.

This completely reverses a very common criticism of religious reasons. They are often dismissed in public discourse for being arbitrary and impossible to substantiate. If this essay is correct, only theism can account for the reliability of *any* of our capacities for moral reasoning. It is non-religious reasoners who must take a more substantial leap of faith: for, on a secular account, it is a matter of inexplicable good fortune that the faculties which generate our moral convictions manage to track the truth.

When taken together with other Theos publications, this essay provides a wide-ranging response to the 'New Atheist' campaign to exclude religious reasons from any role in shaping public policy. Religious perspectives need not be divisive, reactionary *or* irrational. They are capable of rational engagement and evaluation. In a pluralist society, religious and non-religious citizens will need to engage in both apologetic argument (seeking to persuade others that their worldview is correct) and more pragmatic negotiation (seeking to build a common life with others in the midst of ongoing disagreements on moral issues, including political questions). *All* democratic politics involves that mixture of different kinds of deliberation. It requires both rational argument and pragmatic negotiation, and religious worldviews can be as hospitable to rational engagement as secular ones. Indeed, as we have seen, theism best explains why this process of deliberation is reliable at all.

chapter 3 references

1   See B. J. Carr and M. Rees, 'The Anthropic Cosmological Principle and the Structure of the Physical World', *Nature* 278 (12 April 1979), pp. 605-12; and R. Collins, 'Evidence for Fine-Tuning', in Neil A. Manson (ed.), *God and Design: The Teleological Argument and Modern Science* (London: Routledge, 2003), pp. 178-99.

2   Cf. Carl Hempel 'Explanation in Science and in History', in David-Hillel Ruben, *Explanation* (Oxford: Oxford University Press, 1993), pp. 17–41.

3   Charles Taylor, *The Explanation of Behaviour* (London: Routledge & Kegan Paul, 1964), p. 9.

4   See for example Paul M. Churchland, 'Folk Psychology and the Explanation of Behaviour', *Proceedings of the Aristotelian Society*, supp. vol. 62, 1988, pp. 209-21 and Patricia Churchland, *Neurophilosophy* (Cambridge, MA: MIT Press, 1986). For a riposte arguing for an ineliminable role of agent-explanations, see Frank Jackson and Philip Pettit, 'In Defence of Folk Psychology', *Philosophical Studies*, Vol. 57, 1990, pp. 7-30. In my view, this form of reductionism is deeply flawed, but that is outside the scope of this report. An argument for thinking that the Churchlands' worldview is self-defeating is given in Ralph Walker's paper on 'Transcendental Arguments against Physicalism' in Howard Robinson (ed.), *Arguments against Physicalism* (Oxford: Oxford University Press, 1997).

5   At this point, an objector may advance Euthyphro's dilemma: Does God do things because they are good, or are they good because God does them? In *From Morality* pp. 165ff, I argue that theism avoids this dilemma, if it grounds goodness in the loving nature of God.

6   Cf. John Leslie, *Value and Existence* (Oxford: Blackwell, 1979).

7   Hugh Rice, *God and Goodness* (Oxford: Oxford University Press, 2000).

8   Ritchie, *From Morality*, chapter 8.

9   Thomas Nagel's forthcoming book argues for a form of natural teleology – that is, a creative purpose in the universe without a personal God – partly because of the inability of atheistic construals of natural selection to account for moral knowledge. He draws heavily on arguments by Sharon Street in her 'A Darwinian Dilemma for Realist Theories of Value' in *Philosophical Studies* 127 (1), pp. 109-66. See Thomas Nagel, *Mind and Cosmos: Why the Materialist Neo-Darwinian Conception of Nature Is Almost Certainly False* (Oxford: Oxford University Press, forthcoming).

10 Christian faith is not usually – if ever – the conclusion of an intellectual argument. I discuss the role of such arguments in the life of faith in *From Morality*, pp. 189-90. This draws heavily on John Paul II, *Faith and Reason—Fides et Ratio* (London: Catholic Truth Society, 1998).